The First Little Bastard to Call Me Gramps

Poems of the Late Middle Ages

The First Little Bastard to Call Me Gramps

Poems of the Late Middle Ages

Bill Richardson

Illuminated by
Roxanna Bikadoroff

ANANSI

Published in Canada in 2015 by House of Anansi Press Inc.

House of Anansi Press
110 Spadina Avenue, Suite 801
Toronto, ON, M5V 2K4
Tel. 416-363-4343
Fax 416-363-1017
www.houseofanansi.com

House of Anansi Press is committed to protecting our natural environment.
As part of our efforts, the interior of this book is printed on paper that contains
100% post-consumer recycled fibres, is acid-free, and is processed chlorine-free.

19 18 17 16 15   1 2 3 4 5

Library and Archives Canada Cataloguing in Publication

Richardson, Bill, 1955-, author
The first little bastard to call me Gramps : poems of the late
middle ages / Bill Richardson ; Roxanna Bikadoroff, illustrator.

Issued in print and electronic formats.
ISBN 978-1-4870-0054-7 (bound).—ISBN 978-1-4870-0056-1 (html)

I. Title.

PS8585.I186F57 2015   C811'.54   C2015-902105-7
                           C2015-902106-5

Book design: Alysia Shewchuk
Cover and interior illustrations: Roxanna Bikadoroff

*We acknowledge for their financial support of our publishing program the Canada
Council for the Arts, the Ontario Arts Council, and the Government of Canada
through the Canada Book Fund.*

Printed and bound in Canada

For Stan — BR
For Joe — RB

Then Speech was mannerly, an Art,
Like learning not to belch or fart:
I cannot settle which is worse,
The Anti-Novel or Free Verse.

—W.H. Auden,
"Doggerel by a Senior Citizen"

Admittedly, I err by undertaking
This in its present form. The baldest prose
Reportage was called for, that would reach
The widest public in the shortest time.

—James Merrill,
"The Book of Ephraim"

CONTENTS

LONG, LONG AGO

I still remember vividly
The day that it occurred,
The fresh-faced gas attendant,
The first to call me "Sir."
"Can I fill you up, sir?"
He tended to my tank.
I almost spewed my coffee,
I almost choked on "Thanks."

I was thirtysomething then,
And he was seventeen:
Oh, the intervening years,
The things he must have seen.
He's forty in the shade now:
That dude's a "Sir" himself,
With fewer years before him
Than rest upon the shelf.

I'm sure he never thinks of me
As now I think of him
While taking inventory
Of a stock that's growing grim.
My hairline's past receding.
My teeth are end of term.
My chest is strangely sunken.
My gut has left the firm.

And south of the equator,
Within its nest of white,
Reclines the flaccid spigot
I empty thrice a night.
I'm well inured to "Sir" now,
What's next, I know full well,
But the first little bastard to call me Gramps
Gets bitch-slapped straight to hell.

THE GENTLEMAN'S ORACLE

Q:
"Tell me, O wise one,
Tell me, I pray,
Tell me when old age begins."

A:
"It begins on the morning
Your mirror discloses
Your scrotum and face are now twins."

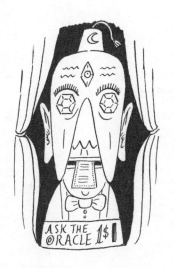

REALITY CHECK

This bromide that one ought to "follow one's bliss"
Is an adage that merits inspection:
Chances are good in your fifties you'll find
That your bliss has no sense of direction.

THE M-WORD

I'm sorry, but were you just talking to me?
　　You seemed to be, so I don't understand
Your aberrant choice of that cruel honorific,
By which, sonny-boy, I mean "Ma'am."

"Do you need some help out with your groceries,
　　Ma'am?"
I'm fairly persuaded that's what I heard.
I'm pretty convinced it was me in your crosshairs
Just now when you used the M-word.

For starters, my lad, I've just come from the gym,
Where my reign as "Free Weight Queen" is secure.
So porting my purchases isn't a problem,
That much I can tell you for sure.

And just who is this "Ma'am" to whom you refer?
That's what I'm needing to parse and construe.
It's a rite of passage all women must weather,
But why here and now? Why with you?

What are you seeing that makes me Ma'am-worthy?
Why, all at once, do I merit that name?
Are my eyelids flaccid? Have my crow's feet deepened?
Are roots the root cause of this shame?

Ma'am.
       Ma'am.
              Ma'am.

Has a less appealing word ever been coined?
Ma'am. It suggests some lamentable creature,
A retiring Sunday school superintendent
Or former piano teacher.

As phonemes go, Ma'am is so unattractive.
It ought to be struck from contractions of speech:
It's the bleat of a lamb at the abattoir gates,
A labouring goat who's in breech.

Your name tag reveals that you are called Barry.
Barry, I'm Mary. I'm glad we've spoken.
If you can remember the things I've just told you,
Your nose will remain unbroken.

You seem a sweet kid and I think it's likely
You trod the path of errant invective
Having taken to heart some head office memo,
Or manager's dumb directive.

If that's so, Barry, question authority!
Never say "Ma'am"! Tamp it down! Take a pass!
That's all. Sayonara. We're done here. We're
    finished.
Except to say, Barry, nice ass.

THE NIGHT WE FOUND THE RIDING CROP

Annabelle came last weekend to visit. Her mother, our daughter, Kate, had the excellent sense to marry a geek. Their lives have turned out great.

As newlyweds, they installed themselves in a "funky, boho loft." A few months later, his start-up bonbon was swallowed by Microsoft. (I never quite understood what it was, though I easily grasped the results: ten verdant acres, devotion to leisure, though sometimes, for fun, he "consults.")

They've plenty of time to refine their lifestyles. Hence Katie, last week, on the phone, with news of their "marriage renewal weekend"; hence Annabelle, coming on loan. Lordy, we had such a marvellous time, telling stories far into the night, of the olden days, when fridges had frost and TVs were — gasp! — black and white.

We were pleased, as always, to see her, of course, the better for us to ensure that our granddaughter has the occasion to study the lives of the working poor (which opportunity never befalls her when hanging about with her chums: a privileged set from a private school with an "equine curriculum"). Annabelle always dresses the part, in jodhpurs, her *casquette* on top; and that explains how we have, in our keeping, her spanking-new riding crop.

When Kate and her mate came to pick up their daughter, when all the goodbyes had been said, we two, in tidying Annabelle's room, discovered it under the bed. The whip was beside a vocational volume, *For Girls Who Aspire to Be Vets*: forbidding, and rigid, and redolent, slightly, of leather and horseflesh, and sweat.

Jeff—he's my husband—said, "Lou! Look at this!" and playfully whacked at my flank. "Bad boy!" I chided, then grabbed it and rendered a rather more serious spank. Tit turned to tat, and this became that, and—pardon me, if I wax coarse—soon we were vying for who'd be the jockey and who'd be the whinnying horse. The fly on the wall saw two neophyte flagellants frolic with lick and with flick. No rod was spared and the yelps in the air were old dogs, acquiring new tricks.

Kate phoned next morning and made passing mention of Annabelle's mounting distress. The crop was her favourite. By chance, had we found it? My answer, I fear, was not "Yes." A lie? Yes, a lie. There's no doubt about it. I'll neither explain nor defend it. We've kindled the fuel of our marriage renewal. Try it. We both recommend it.

A LITTLE BIT PISSED AT DEE DEE

It isn't really her fault, I guess,
The reason is doubtless genetic;
But always, when we go out in a group,
The rest of us end up splenetic.
We go to a gallery, go to a play,
Go somewhere where we'll be regarded
As worthy of discount because of our age,
And Dee Dee's the one who gets carded.

"What? You? Sixty-five? You can't be that old.
Let's see some identification."
Then comes the reveal. She's seventy-two.
"Noxzema and proper hydration,"
Dee Dee replies when, as always, she's grilled
On her secret for staying so frisky,
Though we know very well she has stashed in
    her purse
Her Camels and flagon of whisky.

The worst of it is, she isn't a bitch.
She's vibrant! She's funny! She twinkles!
Dear God, I feel shabby to link in my prayers
Her name—i.e., Dee Dee—with wrinkles.
When dawns the dire day she abandons life's lease,
When her tenancy here is relinquished,
She'll look half her age in her plush, open casket,
At peace, and uncreased, and extinguished.

PROGRESS

Jenny's learning numbers.
I held her up to see
The robins in our birdbath.
She counted, "One, two, three."

Later on, we wandered
Along the sandy shore.
"Count the shells," I told her.
She did. "One, two, three, four."

I tucked her in at bedtime.
She looked up with a grin.
"Five," she said, while tallying
The offspring of my chin.

Next day, at the public pool,
An even crueller cut.
"Six," she said. Her census
Was the roll call of my gut.

Jenny is my grandchild.
Jenny's smart and sweet.
Now she's mastered numbers,
We'll start working on "discreet."

THE NEWS CYCLE

A baby is expected,
A little girl arrives.
They name the child Miranda:
She's one, she's three, she's five.
She's talking, walking, running.
She learns to read, to spell.
She's good at mathematics,
At track and field as well.
Grade three, grade five, grade seven,
First kiss, first broken heart.
Grades nine, ten, and eleven,
A Bachelor of Arts.
Employment, marriage, children,
A silver hair appears:
The usual bewildering
Trajectory of years.

Betrayal, separation,
Her husband's web of lies,
Their reconciliation
Short-lived and ill-advised.
A new-found independence,
Flirtations, torrid trysts:
Miranda's late-life stable
Of "friends with benefits."
A lump, a twinge, a gnawing.
The verdict: very ill.
Miranda sees her lawyer,
Miranda makes her will.
She rallies. She's determined.
She won't concede defeat.
She holds her first great-grandchild:
The bucket list, complete.
Her book club's monthly meeting:
Miranda doesn't show.
"Too bad about Miranda.
You mean, you didn't know?"

PYRRHIC ONEIRIC LYRIC

His first erotic stirrings were for Princess Margaret Rose,
The sister of Elizabeth, the Queen of all the Realm.
Margaret, in his reveries, was *"vraiment quelque chose"*:
The pilot of his dream-time boat, the tiller at his helm.

Every night he'd close his eyes and Margaret would arrive,
And every night they'd caper till the rosy blush of dawn,
And every night he'd take her to a ball, or on a drive,
His cherished Cinderella, but with both her slippers on.

He'd sometimes dare to kiss her as they walked in Regent's Park,
Or else they might brush fingertips while dining at the Ritz.
He carved their twinned initials deep in Sherwood Forest bark,
And held her in his arms while they took shelter from the Blitz.

Now, in the name of probity, one ought to make it plain
That these excursions livened up his prepubescent nights,
And never did their frolicking give way to telltale stain,
Nor did he ever spread his wings in onanistic flight.

Such days of hot, unbridled spill, of course, would soon intrude,
Would supersede their grave gavotte with crude, salacious dance.
But Margaret was unsullied by such sallies with the lewd:
That was Ava Gardner's role, and, just once, Cary Grant's.

That was fifty years ago. He'd put it from his mind,
Until, unbidden, Margaret Rose returned again to haunt
The halls of his nocturnal manse. He shut his eyes to find
Her waiting, as in times of old, a royal revenant.

She's very well preserved for one who's been consigned to earth,
She cuts a cunning figure in her gown/tiara mix.
She whispers, "Death contains no *r*, and darling, there's no dearth
Of pleasures here abounding on the dark side of the Styx.

"Come join me, love," she whispers, then looks glum when he
    demurs,
And puts on hold the moment of their ectoplasmic mesh.
He'll never rush to take his place among the long interred
When there's the slightest chance he'll met Kate Middleton in
    the flesh.

JOANIE TALKS BACK TO THE RADIO

To the gentleman touting
the various virtues
of three-dimensional printing,
breathlessly telling us that—
in addition to widgets
and gizmos and screws—
we'll also be able
to copy our organs,
replace them in manner unstinting,
and live to a hundred and twenty,
well, buddy,
please pardon my French,
but fuck you.

DEAR SIR OR MADAM

As President of the Fifty Plus Club, with our
branches all over the nation, I'm fully engaged in a
constant review of the status of all applications. On
behalf of the board, then, I'm pleased to inform you
your membership's now been approved; this letter
confirms that all liens and impediments forthwith
are stricken, removed. We've vetted credentials,
checked out your references, deemed you as fully
admissible, so now we can send you, by registered
parcel, the cloak that will make you invisible.

The Cloak of Invisibility! Some believe that
they'll never adjust to it, but once you have passed
through the portal of fifty, you'd bloody well better
get used to it. No need to fret over ardent admirers
making unwanted advances: you can wander the
streets in your jammies and slippers and not even
get second glances. You might, now and then, feel
a wee bit bewildered at losing your sexual currency.
You might feel a pang for the days of your youth,
for those frequent frenzies of fervency. But you'll

find that in time you'll adapt to this state of an ever-increasing opacity. True, you're obscure, but you're nonetheless sure you're acquiring a fresh perspicacity: for deep in your being, the sheepdog called Ageing has over the decades been herding a whole flock of interests you never heard bleating, like knitting and Scrabble and birding.

It's part of God's plan: it's bountiful, merciful, not, as it seems, reprehensible, that once in our fifties, we say, "Ix-nay, Fashion," and start to buy shoes that are sensible—rubber-soled shoes that are water-resistant, shoes that we would have found risible; birdwatching shoes, badly wrought, misbegotten, but who the hell cares? You're invisible! (And being invisible counts for a lot, after all, now you're deeply invested in tramping around in the woods madly peering for anything banded or crested.)

Dear Sir or Madam, dear Madam or Sir, to the Fifty Plus Club you're admitted. Make an appointment to bring in your cloak, and we'll see that it's properly fitted. You're one of us now, there's no going back: till death do us part, you're a resident. I can't say, "I'll see you," because I won't see you.

My very best wishes,

The President

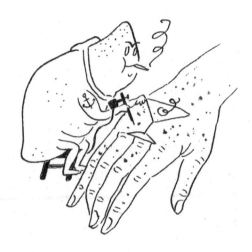

LIVER SPOTS

My liver has mottled my hands with a message
Extending from nails to wrist:
"Bartender, get me another martini,
Dry, and straight up, with a twist."

AS IF

Still, but rarely, there are mornings like this:
The cat neglects to make her wake-up call,
Her ritualized lingual anointing,
Enabling you to find out how this dream —
This matinal, end-of-REM (REMnant?) dream,
Your recurring dream of, blush, tap dancing —
Plays out. You are a star. You are Astaire.
You've taken the chore out of Terpsichore.
You are a paradiddle miracle,
Riff walk sensei and ball change avatar.
The audience in the hall (Carnegie)
Rises as one, plies you with ovations.
Oh, *veni, vidi, saltavi, vici!*
Or something similar along those lines.
Noting that you're among the quick, the cat
Steers the conversation towards breakfast.

You rise. The mood persists. Nietzschean angst
Gives way to brainless, Enid Blyton cheer,
To a groundless, unfounded jollity,
As if the Governor himself has made
A personal call to your death row cell
With his letter of clemency, as if
A genie said, "What the hell. Have a fourth.
Who's counting?," as if the oncologist
Bears truffles and news of benignity,
As if a chorus line of unicorns

Is waiting down the block, farting rainbows,
As if you've learned in your sleep to play bridge,
And the bassoon. There are mornings like this
Still, but rarely; and surely as kittens
Become cats, mornings become afternoons.

NOBLESSE OBLIGE

Commendable, those who cede nothing to age
And who run when the Marathon whistles.
Out in their singlets and satiny shorts,
All lean meat, and sinew and gristle.
Up in the morning and downing a smoothie
Of yogurt and flaxseed and dulse,
Then pounding the pavement bedight with devices
For measuring mileage and pulse.

If wishes were horses, I'd run with that pack,
But the dress code's so very debasing.
Swaddled in Lycra, I look like a sausage
Inexpertly stuffed in its casing.
So here is my customized fitness plan:
Though I'll never have triceps like timbers,
Cocktail shaking engenders a sweat
And my wrists are incredibly limber.

STRIP MALL

Antiquity's imperatives: by now, I know them well.
My old dogs need some low-fat food that only vets can sell.

The clinic's in a strip mall—mostly closed and shuttered stores—
Though, latterly, a dim sum joint has opened up next door.

(Our neighbourhood is fractured, but a cheerful unanimity
Derives from sophomoric jokes concerning this proximity,

A coprophagous catalogue of cruder, crude, and crudest.)
So I could check "buy kibble" off my supersized to-do list,

I fired up the Honda, drove, and claimed a vacant spot
Adjacent to a Prius in the nearly vacant lot.

I let the engine idle, lingered in the car to hear
A symphony I've known and loved for nearly fifty years,

Mahler's Fourth, the final movement: *Das himmlische Leben*.
James Levine, Chicago, with soprano Judith Blegen.

(Not quite on my A-list; I prefer, though no one's asking,
Szell conducting Cleveland with soprano Judith Raskin.)

"Life in Heaven sure is grand," the angel smugly sings,
Riding the sustaining drone of klezmer-coloured wings.

The English horn and basses bring the movement to an end.
I jacked the volume up to hear that bowed and low amen.

Coincident, bizarre but true, with that decaying dirge,
I looked towards the clinic door and from it saw emerge

A couple, round about my age — my birth year's '55 —
The owners of the Prius was my high-IQ surmise.

They clung to one another as they walked across the lot.
He was pale and stoic, she was visibly distraught.

Her knees gave way. He grabbed her arm. He stopped to help
    her stand,
And that was when I saw the leather collar in his hand.

Strip mall clinic. Public mourning. Dog and collar schism.
Sophocles! Emergency! A nascent syllogism!

All those years of walking, grooming, gathering up the shit,
And now this empty parking lot, this tragedy, small writ.

"Oh God, oh God," I said, reluctant witness to their pain.
I muttered, "Oh, sweet Jesus Christ," and then, "Oh, God," again.

He searched his pockets, found his keys, depressed the willing
    fob.
Our two looks locked as locks unlocked. We shared a manly
    nod.

Slam of doors, and turn of key, and subtle purr of hybrid.
Blasting from their speakers came the twerksome Miley
Cyrus.

Rossini on the CBC had pulled the rug from Mahler.
I watched them leave, that couple with the cooling, empty
collar.

"Soon, that will be me," I thought, as always solipsistic.
Then flayed myself with psychic whips for being narcissistic.

The vet's disgorged a new-spayed dog, weighed down by
telltale cone.
I went inside. I bought the food. I left. I headed home.

NEVER DOUBT THE TRUTH WILL OUT

We were sad about Ted and Muriel,
And surprised to learn they were gone.
Muriel died on Tuesday at dusk,
And Ted died on Wednesday at dawn.
Aggrieved though we were,
We could also see
That in death, at times,
There is poetry.

It was like it was scripted, foreordained,
As if some angelic force planned
And choreographed their departure:
They exited, hand clutching hand.
For fifty-six years
A couple, best friends,
A solid-state unit
Entwined till the end.

The memorial service was lovely.
The trouble with winding up dead
Is missing the unctuous tributes
Like Muriel garnered, and Ted.
Ted was eulogized,
Likewise Muriel.
Gosh, how we miss them.
Now, the burial.

Conspicuous during the obsequies
Was Captain Popcorn, their parrot:
Old as the hills, a bawdy macaw,
Partial to parsnips and carrots.
The priest said, "Amen,"
Then opened the mike,
So anyone there
Could say what they liked.

Second to dying, it's often been said,
In the dread-and-loathing spectrum,
Is public speaking: just the prospect
Wrenches a clench from the rectum.
An awkward silence
Suffusing the church
Till Captain Popcorn
Made pulpit of perch.

"You know you shouldn't be driving at night."
"You know I can't stomach canned peas."
"For God's sake, Ted, remember your pills."
"Hey, Muriel, where are my keys?"
"You're mumbling again."
"There's hair in the sink."
"There's booze on your breath."
"Christ, give me a drink."

"Rabbits, Muriel, like to eat salads,
  But men have a passion for meat."
"For God's sake, Ted, can you wipe the rim?
  Can you flush and lower the seat?"
"You can't cook a roast—
  My ma had the knack."
"Then go straight to hell
  And bring the bitch back."

The moral, I guess, if one there must be,
Is nothing is as it appears.
They'd always seemed so sugary sweet.
They weren't. That was perfectly clear.
Look under the rock:
Amazing what squirms.
I wish we had sprung
For more than one urn.

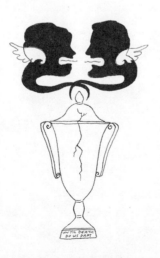

DAY PLANNER

5 a.m.

You wake up short of breath,
Your heart begins to race.
It's not approaching death:
The cat is on your face.
You sneeze and hack and blow.
You slide beneath the covers.
Was it so long ago
You shared your bed with lovers?

7 a.m.
Coffee: Drink.
Paper: Read.
Wrist: Check.
Pulse? Proceed.

9 a.m.

Catalogue the reasons why you'll quit this life or stay,
And if the list is favouring "can't take it anymore,"
Remember Thursday coming up is Seniors' Discount Day
At your local pharmacy and wholesale pet food store.

11 a.m.

Remember what the sages say:
it's later than you think.
Skype your friend in Tokyo,
and join him for a drink.

1 p.m.
Your tongue is a tad on the fuzzy side,
You're feeling a little unsteady.
Two is the time that you're slated to nap:
You'd better lie down and get ready.

3 p.m.
You're feeling a long way from certain,
Your back and your ankles are sore.
Why bother to open the curtains?
There's no need to rise before four.

5 p.m.
"Exercise." The word's a ghost
Of faint, grey graphite traces.
Praise the lord for pencil
Which so readily erases.

7 p.m.
Cook yourself a vegan meal with what's on hand
in fridge and bin.
Are chips considered vegetables?
Of course they are, and so is gin.

9 p.m.
Another stab at *Moby-Dick*:
Five minutes in, you hurl
The bloody book across the room
And watch *The Golden Girls*.

11 p.m.
Turn out the lights and climb the stairs,
Moisturize and say your prayers.
You're agnostic, true, but yet
It never hurts to hedge your bets.

1 a.m.

You dream that you're limber, attractive, and happy,
You dream that your days are uncluttered, unfraught,
You dream till you wake and take stock of the present:
What's true when you're dreaming, when waking is not.

3 a.m.

Stare at the ceiling
while trying to choose:
Which would you rather,
coach tour or cruise?

CHOICES, CHOICES

Let us be frank. Let's be perfectly clear:
We all must re-enter the biosphere.
We all must relinquish the ghost one day,
Forsaking the clutch of the festering clay.
No one, post-mortem, can linger ambrosial:
Redolence renders us highly disposable.
When you've come to the end of your fro-ing
    and to-ing,
Will it be planting or will it be strewing?
Stoking the furnace or pickled and binned?
Two metres under or gone with the wind?
Men in tall hats with a box made of timber,
Or some sort of urn that's a condo for cinders?
Your ashes consigned to a rippling gulch,
Or bones, flesh and viscera turning to mulch?
It's like, if you want my considered surmise,
That old blue-plate quandary of "Salad or fries?"
Some opt for plantable, some favour roastable.
Whatever! The sum of our parts is compostable.

PRAYER

You'll know, if you've been to a nursing home,
That when choirs of children come in,
For reasons in no way apparent to me,
They're compelled to include Vera Lynn.

It's never Bill Haley, the Drifters, Paul Anka;
If someone can answer, pray tell,
Why nightingales singing in Berkeley Square?
Why never once "Heartbreak Hotel"?

When my time finally comes for the Shady Vale,
When my life is essentially over,
Can we have "Satisfaction," and maybe "Hey Jude,"
And to hell with "The White Cliffs of Dover"?

STRANGE IDYLL

My mother's in a nursing home that's called the
Pleasant Grove. Her well-stocked mind has latterly
become a pillaged trove. I'll find her in her dressing
gown. She'll look up and exclaim some random
appellation, always someone else's name.

I've sometimes been her brother, whom we
scattered near Palm Beach, or stood in for her
cousin, who is likewise out of reach. I've also been
her lawyer, and—by far the most bizarre—the
chatty Mrs. Godfrey, who was Mother's weekly char.
(The diatribe she loosed that day on sainted Mrs. G,
who chipped a precious gravy boat in 1963.)

Today, I brought her flowers. Her mood was blithe
and gay. "How precious, Fred," she giggled as she
reached for my bouquet. By Fred, she meant her
husband; my pa, that is, was Fred. He left us sixty
years ago, to dwell among the dead. A sporting
mishap took him the winter I turned three: my ma
was made a widow by a ski hill and a tree.

For me, he was a photograph: dead Fred upon the
shelf. I'd study it and look in vain for traces of myself.
Nothing in our features spoke of two peas in a pod,
nor did I look like Ma: I was genetically at odds.
They were dark and I am blond. I grew beyond six
feet; Pa was five foot five and Ma bought frocks
from Miss Petite.

"How precious, Fred," she giggled as a blend of
fragrant bloom and bitter antiseptic wound its way
around the room. "I'm very fond of freesias, don't
they make a splendid show? Oh Freddy, dear, I'm
glad you're here, there's something you should know.

"I've tried and tried to tell you, Fred —" Her face
was plaintive, glum. "I'll just come out and say it.
Darling, Michael's not your son. It's been my darkest
secret, love, so painful to endure. Oh, say you love
me still," she said. I gulped and stammered, "Sure."

"I know you've always wondered, I know you've had
a hunch. I know —" And then the nurse came in.
She said, "It's time for lunch."

"Lunch!" cried Ma. "Hooray, I'm starved." Said nurse,
"Then best get dressed. Is this your son? Perhaps he'll
stay and join you as your guest."

"My son?" she said. She looked confused, then
understanding dawned. "Michael, love." She stood
and hugged her tall, illicit spawn.

At lunch, she seemed her former self: a gracious,
charming host. I ate my meal, and most of hers:
chipped beef on whole wheat toast. I tried to keep
my focus, but I couldn't help recall the egg man,
who was Danish, fair, and very, very tall.

Nap time came. We said goodbye. I said I'd be back
soon. Driving home, I thought about the loveliness
of ruins. O, Parthenon! O, Ephesus! Pompeii!
Medusa's Raft! I made a fist. I punched the horn. I
laughed. I cried. I laughed.

OUR MUTABLE FRIEND

Some beliefs are carved in stone,
Some standards are past assailing.
I know my mind:
I'm one of those
Who all my life
Has been opposed
To oil refining,
Surface mining,
Leghold traps
And whaling.
What's more, I always
Thought I'd be
Averse to plastic surgery.
But something's changed.
I've felt a shift.
The famous clinic
Of Tuck and Lift
Looks more and more appealing.

No commandment says, "Thou shalt
Go out a wrinkled martyr."
One risks no
Moral turpitude
By pumping up
The pulchritude.
Shadows lightened,
Cheekbones heightened,
Liver spots
Bleached paler;
Fix up the exterior
From wattles
To posterior.
Bye-bye, eye bags
Hung like sporrans:
If one can look like
Sophia Loren,
Why settle for Norman Mailer?

COMMANDMENTS FOR
THE NEWLY OLD

(The cauldron of archaeology has been thoroughly
shaken and stirred by tablets from Mount Sinai that
were latterly disinterred. For thousands of years we
were led to believe that Ten Commandments were
plenty, but God, hearing rumours of burgeoning
boomers, decided we ought to have twenty.)

11. Thou *Shalt Not* channel "Daytona" whilst thou putts about on thine scooter.

12. Thou *Shalt Not* fake dementia and go wandering, "lost," into Hooters.

13. Thou *Shalt Not* ever stoop to say "the trouble with thine generation."

14. Thou *Shalt*, gents, foist on nose and ears assiduous depilation.

15. When clerks or servers call thee "dear," thou *Shalt Not* answer, "Shove it."

16. That Xbox is thine grandson's, so hands off: thou *Shalt Not* covet.

17. Thou *Shalt Not* say, "Thou callst that music?" or "Please, turn down thine racket."

18. Thou *Shalt* be a tender, loving spouse; thou *Shalt Not* buy matching jackets.

19. Thine surgeries are thine surgeries: with news of them, be sparing.

20. Joint pain is thine private thing, but joints thou *Shalt* be sharing.

LETTER TO A GRANDSON

Here is the principal difference, dude,
I see between me and you:
Your mommy has what mine never had —
Twelve piercings, and six tattoos.

As to the former, her armoured ears
Were a more than sufficient hint;
Likewise, the tongue stud that I mistook
For a Tic Tac or some other mint.

But we only discerned your mommy sports
The tats my mommy lacked
On the day she wed your dad, our son:
Her gown, bereft of a back,

Revealed that her B-side was colonized
By a twisting, tendril vine.
"And what in the world," your granny asked,
"Can be snaking up her spine?"

"Ummm — I'm pretty sure it's a snake," I said,
In a reverential hush,
Surveying the glistening python
Climbing upwards from her tush.

Then, seven months later, you came along,
And now you are nearly four.
You walk and you talk and you hanker
For the world beyond the door,

A marvellous world, if rather more fraught
Than it was when I was young:
When Mommy just wore a bit of blush
And nobody pierced their tongue.

DEAR FRIENDS

I'm so excited that everyone's coming for dinner
next Saturday night! I hope you don't mind me
writing like this, as a kind of pre-emptive strike. I
love how the chatter, when we're all together, will
bubble and ripple and spill, but would it be possible,
when we are eating, to sidestep the subject of pills?

May I request we agree as a group on imposing
a wholesale proscription on anything having
to do with our ailments and all the resultant
prescriptions? It's not that I want you to feel
constrained, and please don't hold anything back,
but can we agree, while you're under my roof, to a
"no pharmaceuticals" pact?

Can we agree you won't lay on the table the
drugs from your bountiful store, and then,
ostentatiously, one by one, take them, explaining
what each one is for? Blood pressure, estrogen,
gastrointestinal, lipids and antidepressants: I'll be
cooking all day, so please bring an appetite, set
aside any suppressants.

It shouldn't require an effort of will, I think not much more than a smidgen, to file Pathology under Verboten, with Politics next to Religion. Let's get together to eat and to drink past the point of all sane satiation; let's leave suppositories where they belong, which is out of the conversation.

I'm so looking forward to seeing you all and to having you here in my home, but please leave your colonoscopy videos closely confined to your phones. Thanks for complying, I'll see you all soon, and if anyone reads this and panics, don't fret, I'll be serving my signature cocktail: gin, with Campari and Xanax.

ROUND ABOUT THREE IN THE MORNING

Never, not once, in your sixty long years,
Never, not once, did you think
It would turn out like this: you'd be living alone,
And eating ice cream, at the sink.

Eating ice cream at the sink, from the tub—
No need to dirty a dish—
Eating ice cream, growing more and more certain
You've wasted your third and last wish.

You look out the window: your ghostly reflection,
Your face like a pocked, puffy moon.
The ice cream is done. You find the Nutella.
You pad off to bed with a spoon.

WHY, OH, WHY?

It's one of life's dunning conundrums,
As tough as the puzzle by Rubik:
Why must the hair that extrudes from our skulls
Go thin, then go white, then go pubic?

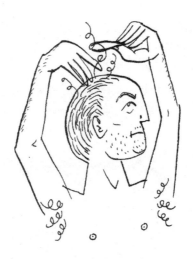

FRIDAY NIGHT

It doesn't mean you've abandoned all hope,
Or fallen to torpor and lethargy,
If when all is done,
If when all is said,
If it's chilly outside,
If it's cozy in bed,
If the dog's at your side,
If the cat's on your head,
You're content to stay home watching *Jeopardy*.

(EXACT) CHANGE IS CERTAIN

At a given moment in any life, in the seventh-
    decade range,
You feel the surge
Of a desperate urge,
Of an urge surpassing strange:
That terrible compulsion for exactitude of change.

There's no epidemiologist who can parse or discern
    or trace
The way it starts.
You wheel your cart
To the cash and take your place,
Not suspecting contagion's claimed you, you're the
    latest case.

It batters your defences down, it circumvents free will.
You'll think you're spared,
You're unimpaired;
Perhaps you are until
It grabs you by the gullet while you're standing at
    the till.

The cashier says, "Six seventy-three," and you
    extract a ten
From among the cash
In your billfold's stash.
You're about to pay, but then
You pause in the proceedings, scratch your head,
    and think again.

"I believe I can do it exactly," you say, as the impulse
    starts to creep.
Among stray mints
And bits of lint
In your pockets, digging deep,
You excavate your random change and pile it in a heap.

"I'm sure I've got it here," you say, as on you plumb
    and delve.
You've been transformed,
Rejigged, reborn,
Sloughed off your former selves,
As though you've saved for this pork chop since
    about the age of twelve.

There's a swell of susurration from the wretches in
    your line.
They shuffle, sigh,
They roll their eyes,
They showily check the time.
The queue's grown exponentially, from three to six
    to nine.

Your coin's all strewn on the counter now, you've
    no more to divest.
Less than brisk,
You've amply frisked
Your trousers, your coat, your vest.
"Seven cents short," the cashier says. She's
    supremely unimpressed.

"Six seventy-three," she says, and then, "Six seventy-
    three" once more.
You want to melt
Or else just pelt
And beat it out the door.
You gather your insufficient change. You spill it on
    the floor.

Eventually, you'll make it home and pour a
    restoring drink.
You'll toast the halt
Of that grim gestalt;
It's over, or so you think.
You're wrong, my friend. There'll be no end:
    you've passed beyond the brink.

The need for the exact right change has clapped on
    you its lock.
You're done. You're doomed.
You'll be too soon
Like the woman from down the block
Who goes to the store with her coins arranged,
    by type, in sundry socks.

You'll never slip that far, you think, but I predict in
    time
You'll take your turn,
Awake, discern
A system's come to mind:
Black for nickels, striped for quarters, argyle for the
    dimes.

KING OF DENIAL

In retrospect, it's abundantly clear I was more than
a little moronic in thinking there'd been an influx
of workers who hailed from places Hispanic.

In looking back, I can understand that my hatches
were largely unbattened, in grouping the workers
with whom I collided under the rubric of Latin.

In stores and in restaurants, in cafés and clinics,
employees seemed bound by a lingo that just didn't
jibe with their physical features that, by and large,
struck me as Gringo.

Many were blue-eyed, were pale and blond: they
were Nordic in cast and demeanour; but all of
them, when I was tendering cash, would ask of me,
"Are you a *señor*?"

I'm lousy at languages, largely immune to
Berlitz and its polyglot splendours, but I'm not
so inept that I failed to get that the question was
referencing gender.

"Is this not," I would wonder, "self-evident? Is my
grasp on the masculine waning?" But I thought it
would be less than decorous, somehow, to press
them for further explaining:

New country, new language, new terrible tangle of
cultural brambles and thickets. So I grinned and I
nodded, I parried with "*Sí*," and I paid for my meal
or my tickets.

And sometimes, if seized by a garrulous fit, in
a "my house is your house" display, and to make
these new immigrants feel more at home, I would
throw in a hearty "*Olé!*"

This happened dozens and dozens of times before
I'd amassed enough data for the terrible truth to lay
hold of a cudgel and whack at me like a piñata.

OMFG! was the phrase I declaimed when the penny dropped, ditto the peso, not in text shorthand but fully orated and lustily, if I do say so.

How risible that I turned John into Juan and made a Juanita of Hilda, by letting some cortex, or do I mean Cortés, embellish the truth with a tilde.

In the fullness of time, I suppose I'll be able to muster a snicker or giggle at how I maintained my delusional state with a small diacritical squiggle.

A few decades hence, I won't feel the longing to beg for an increase of morphine when telling the story of how, in denial, I somehow imputed a morpheme.

Now, bring on the years! Now, let them all in! I'll take them on, mano-a-mano. Now, bring on the discounts! "Now, are you a senior?" "*Sí, sí, yo soy anciano.*"

69 (AND OTHER UNTENABLE POSITIONS)

The Joy of Sex was published back in 1972.
Then, Louise was in her twenties.
Joy? Oh, boy! Louise had plenty.
It was like that in the seventies,
We'd screw and screw and screw.

Speaking of seventy, as we were, Louise is on the verge.
She'll tally soon three score and ten.
Just one more day remains and then
Her sixties she'll not see again.
Another decade, purged.

Cornelius is her boyfriend, he's her lover, her main squeeze.
He's seventy-two, he's feeling fine,
He drops by with some sparkling wine
To bid farewell to sixty-nine,
Her man, who loves to please.

Conspicuous on the coffee table, laid with pride of place,
Louise displays *The Joy of Sex*,
With pills adjacent to that text:
Viagra (his), her Celebrex,
And Aspirin, just in case.

Louise is feeling frisky by the time the wine is spent.
Now comes the touchy-feely stage:
She hoists the book, locates the page,
And shows Cornelius how her age
Is also an event.

"I'd like to see my sixties out by trying this," she coos.
Cornelius ponders on her plan:
He contemplates the diagram.
He says, "I see. I understand.
Why not? What's there to lose?

"It doesn't seem so hard to grasp. I get the main idea.
 On balance, it appears to me
 It's pretty much Tab A, Slot B,
 Assembly simpler than if we
 Went shopping at Ikea."

Our Kama Sutra neophytes, all jocund, start to jostle.
They'd look, if from above espied,
Like something tossed up by the tide,
With knotted limbs and wrinkly hide,
A rare and scary fossil.

They have themselves a glorious time, en route to wholesale mesh.
They frolic, rollick, caper, play.
They never think of hell to pay
Or that perhaps they'll be betrayed
By fickle, feeble flesh.

What supernatural agency puts carnal play on pause?
Some vengeful fairy, unappeased,
Some prudish demigod, displeased,
Makes Corny's neck seize up and freeze
And locks Louise's jaw.

O, horrible simultaneity! O, dark abyss of hope!
The neighbours, startled by their screams,
Alert a paramedic team,
All hard-edged blokes who think they've seen
It all before — but nope.

What bleak concatenation forged this facial-pelvic squelch?
Louise would happily confide
Were not her mouth pre-occupied.
Compressed champagne rears up inside
And exits as a belch.

They're borne out on a stretcher past some kid who's
    quick to use
His phone to post them to the Web.
Eventually, their fame will ebb,
But now they're viral, they're celebs:
Last count, six million views.

Louise is home and resting now. She's largely on the mend.
She's like Piaf, with no regrets.
She sees life in the pink, you bet.
But *soixante-neuf*? Nyet, nyet, nyet, nyet.
On that account, Amen.

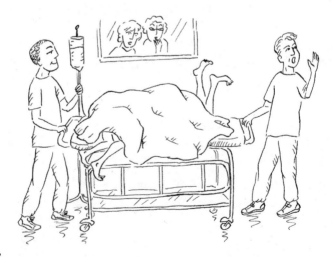

CURT NOTE TO CUTE STRANGER

This is the reason I'm not chipping in
When kidnappers crowd-source your ransom:
To me, just now, "Good morning, sir,"
Just now, to my dog, "Hey there, handsome."

ASTONISHING NEWS FROM LE PAYS DU GROIN

Scientific types who took degrees of high distinction,
PhDs who know a thing or two about extinction,
Reluctantly agreed last night to turf their old surmise.
The Groinland Wolf has not died out:

Surprise,
        Surprise,
                Surprise.

True enough, it's been some years since last the monster
    stirred.
However, inactivity, seems not to mean interred.
Hence, the revelation that the great beast's not yet through.
Late last night, his cry rang out:

Aroo,
        Aroo,
                Aroo.

A howl that made the shepherd rise and hurry to the fold,
A howl that woke the peasantry and made their blood run
    cold,
A howl that also woke my wife, who copped a hurried feel.
"Romeo, it's 3 a.m.:

Get real,
        Get real,
                Get real."

Who could think such savagery would meet such
consternation?
Oh, cruel defeat, oh, swift retreat to winter hibernation.
But this is not the end of him. He'll waken, never fear.
He's primed to prowl. You'll hear him howl

Next year,
Next year,
Next year.

INTERGENERATIONAL

Cynthia's father is sixty-seven,
He's five years a widower now.
He's sworn up and down he'll never remarry.
That is his grief-stricken vow.

Cynthia's son has just turned seventeen.
His licence is hot off the press.
He's got a new car and girlfriend as well:
He's the wellspring of Cynthia's stress.

Cynthia's father, all mopey and lonely,
Was latterly heard to opine
Perhaps he'll endeavour to find a new partner,
Perhaps he'll try dating online.

Cynthia — who is the soul of discretion —
Has wondered, but never inquires,
Whether he's tracked down the digital spark,
The tinder to kindle his fire.

It is Sunday brunch, and Cynthia's father,
Uncharacteristically late,
Gets to the house looking tired and sheepish.
He piles up the eggs on his plate

While Cynthia goes to the stairway and hollers,
"Hey, Jared! The grub's getting cold!"
He joins them, and Cynthia studies her menfolk:
Both tardy, one young and one old.

Her kith and her kin, her blood and her bone,
Are identical in this respect:
The hickeys her father and son are both sporting
The length and the breadth of their necks.

"I am so, so not ready for this," she thinks.
Then, to steady herself, she contrives
To tend to the coffee, allowing the fellows
To smirk and exchange a high-five.

The roar of the coffee mill fails to dampen
The future's intemperate knocking.
Christmas is coming, and Cynthia's planning
The condoms she'll stuff in their stockings.

INDISPENSABILITY

It's one of our favourite fantasies,
A kind of necropolis porn.
We conjure the day
We swoon, pass away,
And leave all our loved ones to mourn.

The sound of their keening is deafening
It echoes from transept to nave.
The garments they're rending
Are well beyond mending
And someone will jump in the grave.

How can it be, when of flesh we're made free
That daylight will follow the dawn?
How can we stand it
To think that the planet
Will spin, on and on, on and on?

But this much I tell you reliably,
Yes, this much is more than a hunch:
Your peers, near and dear,
Might well shed a tear,
But not even one will miss lunch.

INEVITABILITY

When I was an arrogant, callow buck,
I subscribed to a maxim that said
The driver you shouldn't get stuck behind
Is the chap with the cap on his head.

Nothing provoked a coarse "Oh, bloody hell!"
Or else "Jumping Jehoshaphat, no!"
As trying to escape the treacherous wake
Of a slow bloke in tweedy chapeau.

He'd be the one with his foot on the brake,
With the penchant for straddling all lanes:
As if the damn cap was tapping his sap,
And diverting the blood from his brain.

I'd built up empirical evidence
Of this fashion-derived ad hominem;
I'd witnessed it time and time again,
This cap-drives-like-crap sad phenomenon.

Does something genetic render it so?
How fatuous is it to postulate
Some grim biochemical shift occurs
As the prostate gives up and depopulates?

Did God, or whoever, think to install
On the middle-aged man's cluttered console
A switch for the wish to don a tweed cap
And then drive like an absolute asshole?

A week or so back — I can't tell you why —
A perverse, atavistic force surged,
To stop and to visit a Goodwill store.
I succumbed, while therein, to the urge

To seek out a bin, the one labelled Hats,
To rummage about, willy-nilly,
To find there consigned not merely a cap
But somebody's disavowed Tilley.

"Jaunty," I thought, when I tried the thing on,
And then, upon closer inspection,
Added, "And sexy!" Discreetly, I blew
A kiss to my full-length reflection.

I paid fifty cents, I wore the thing out,
I was merry and blithe, but my spark
Extinguished on finding my windshield
    besmirched
With a note that advised, "Learn to park."

True, I had taken two spaces, but still,
Such brutishness wasn't required.
And then, as I made to pull out of the spot,
A cacophonous squealing of tires

Caught me up short. The jerk in the truck
That had made the precipitate stop
Leaned from his window and rudely exclaimed,
"Have you heard about signal lights, Pops?"

I fired right back, an expletive volley,
Laid zinger on zinger on zinger.
We ended our quarrel in the grown-up way,
With a mutual flashing of fingers.

Oh, what an eventful journey back home;
One couldn't but notice and mark it:
The hooting of horns as I sat through the green,
The hollers of "Drive it or park it."

Whatever occurred when Tilley met skull
Was queer, unforeseen, and transformative.
Illegal left turns and one-ways misread:
Now these are utterly normative.

I hear you all call, "Just turf the damn thing!"
How can I? It patiently waited
For me, for the day I'd dig through that bin,
For our union, predestined and fated.

In every man's life, some hat has to fall:
Thus sages and casuists blather.
There's a cap or a Tilley inscribed with your name.
A trophy? No, atrophy, rather.

Life's many inevitabilities!
They keep us at sixes and sevens.
Pardon me now while I parallel park.
This next try is number eleven.

JUST ONE MORE

You're not an idiot. Objectively,
You've known from the get-go this would happen.
You come home from the shelter, the breeder,
From whatever the source of this folly,
And sure as you know your good intentions
About table feeding and couch sharing,
About spoiling and infantilizing,
About that rigorous training regime,
Will within days be wrapped up and mothballed
And stored in whatever sad, unlined drawer
You keep your discarded resolutions;
As sure as this you know, you understand
That you will begin to steady yourself
Against the day when, against the day when—
No. Don't go there. Nihilism, vamoose.
Too late. You've invited the vampire in.

And that thought, once it's thought, will live with you
Always, will inveigle, insinuate
Its way into your dull quotidian,
A kind of low-frequency tinnitus,
The anxious thrum of a labouring fridge.
More and more, out on those three-times-dailies,
You'll be invaded by the certainty
That someone's watching, behind lace curtains,
From some high window. You'll shiver, move on.

You're not an idiot. Objectively,
You've known from the get-go this would happen.
And now it does, in plodding increments.
She misjudges the jump from floor to bed.
Squirrels go unremarked, cats are unassailed.
The bass continuo to her stretching
Has become an attenuated groan.
There are certain lapses in etiquette.
Her penchant for sulphurous off-gassing
Becomes a social liability,
A bit of a conversation stopper
At dinner parties—not that you're inclined
Anymore to willingly engineer
Such gatherings; there are far fresher hells
On which to waste time and money, God knows.

No longer moved to transports of delight
By the turning of your key in the lock,
She yawns at the Old Reliables.
You tell yourself that after all these years
She's turned a corner, come to understand
That dried lamb's liver is dried lamb's liver,
No cause for Dionysian frenzy.
You've googled "Vets Vancouver Home Visits."
You've thought of possible scattering grounds,
Considered the merits of beaches, fields.

You're not an idiot. Objectively,
You've known from the get-go this would happen.
And even though you've assiduously
Girded your loins against the maudlin—
"No, no, Mama! We cain't shoot Ol' Yeller!"—
Nevertheless, you are sure to succumb,
Not just to the cheap and sentimental,
But to the delusional calculus
Of trying to determine if there's time,
Time enough remaining for one more dog,
Just one, just one more. No. You can't. You *cain't*.
Ridiculous, absurd to think of it,

Irresponsible. Consider your age.
If you could do the seven times table,
Which you no longer can, you could measure
It out in dog years, O Methuselah.
My God, if the thing lived for fourteen years,
Then you would be — Well. That seems unlikely.
Never mind. There's one more summer, at least,
To enjoy with the present incumbent
With possibly your last dog. Time will tell.
You woke her last night, running from something,
Your four limbs twitching in dream. Her look said,
"I love you, you drooling, great idiot."
Which, objectively, possibly, you are.

THE THING HE LOVED BEST

It is often said of adrenalin junkies,
after it all goes south —
when they tumble off a rock face,
or their chutes fail to deploy,
or the storm they're chasing turns around
and gathers them in its mouth —
at least they were snuffed while burning bright
with incandescent joy.

I state here and now, I devoutly hope
it will never be said of me,
"He perished doing the thing he loved best."
I should hate to think my loss
will now and forevermore be linked
to an excess of carnal glee:
found unresponsive, clutching a cream puff,
slathered in hot fudge sauce.

SELF-SUFFICIENCY

She'd rise at 4 a.m.
She'd line up in the cold,
The better to ensure her kids were guaranteed a place
At Mrs. Parker's daycare,
Which was, so she'd been told,
The ultimate, with umpteen children vying for each space.

And then, as time went on,
She'd wheedle and connive
For French immersion, music lessons: cunning, her intrigues.
It was worth the effort:
Her children grew and thrived
And went to university, each college Ivy League.

They grew and flew the coop.
They're scattered far and near.
They call their mother weekly, from Toronto, Linz, Japan.
They worry she's declining.
They come home once a year.
They say, "She's surely slipping. We had better make a plan."

How quickly they forget
Her genius for control.
She's done her homework, looked around, and canvassed all
    her cronies.
The Golden Haven's best.
Her name is on the roll,
And no one who has dealt with her can doubt she's got *cojones*.

She's ready for the call.
Her ducks are in a row.
She's waiting for the view room, seventh floor, the northwest
    corner.
She has her spies in place.
She's packed and set to go
The minute Bertha McIntosh is borne out by the coroner.

YOUR MEMORY HAS BEEN RECALLED

Facts were once at your steady command:
A regiment ready and proper.
But now, as the crossword increasingly shows,
They're AWOL, they're truant, they've scarpered.

Who invented the cotton gin?
Who is the brother of Thor?
What is the width of the Rubicon?
How long was the Hundred Years' War?
Who wrote the books about Nero Wolfe?
When were the Fenian Raids?
Chandler and Hammett invented detectives,
But which gave us Marlowe, which Spade?

Facts were once like impeccable dogs:
You whistled, they came, without fail.
Now they just quiver and pee in the hall,
Or run around, chasing their tails.

Are Brussels sprouts properly brassica?
Are fusilli pastas or cheeses?
Barbera — is that a hearty, rich red,
Or the guy on the cross next to Jesus?
A four-letter word meaning "dunkable treat,"
Three letters for "binary digit,"
In nineteen hundred and fifty-nine,
Who starred in the classic film *Gidget*?

Facts once came tumbling, blithesome and light,
They leapt from a mind tightly sprung.
Now you're aware of their terrible weight
As they mass on the tip of your tongue.

The book that precedes Deuteronomy,
The names of the Mexican states,
What *B* and what *W* signify
When, reversed, they're appended to Yeats.
Combustible's eight-letter antonym,
A four-letter word for "elliptic."
And these are the simple, quotidian clues;
Let's not even dwell on the cryptic.

Facts were the plentiful coin of your realm,
But now your brain favours the frugal.
Sweating this small stuff will wrinkle your brow:
The hell with it. Just call up Google.

WE NOW INVITE THE
CONGREGATION TO PAUSE FOR
PRAYER AND MEDITATION

In the space of, it's certain, a very few years
I'll be languishing under the clover,
And I find myself wondering more and more:
Have I fucked my life thoroughly over?
Have I pillaged what started as bountiful,
Have I left it a desperate mess?
Have I always said yes when I should have said no,
And said no when I should have said yes?
How many times, when I should have been glad
For a colleague or friend, was I jealous?
Whence these regrets, in the dead of the night,
I was never a doctor, or cellist?

What's past repairing and what can be fixed?
How best to contend with attrition
Of mental acuity, sexual prowess,
And various half-baked ambitions?
(When finally one has been filed and consigned
To that dank subterranean roost,
Some graveside detractor will sneeringly snicker,
"He never did make it through Proust.")
The Terminus, friends, is a charming hotel
And there's plenty of room at the inn,
And the happy hour goes on and on,
And they've never once run out of gin.

GOD'S PLAN

The presents poured in:
The books and the blankets,
The booties, the bonnets, the bibs,
And eight or nine mobiles,
Inventive, attractive,
For hanging up over the crib.

Artfully dangling from strings
And from wires were
Butterflies, bells, and balloons,
And duckies and fishies
And doggies and kitties
And planets and comets and moons.

Some were quite simple,
They'd bob in the breeze,
While some were made active by winding.
They'd play "Twinkle, Twinkle,"
Or else "Für Elise,"
Or "The Rustle of Springtime" by Sinding.*

The mobiles were meant
To lend to the nursery
An atmosphere calm and bucolic,
But baby, contrary,
Would not be made merry:
His howls raised the spectre of colic.

Mobiles in motion
Created commotion,
His parents were given no peace,
As though in the womb
He'd been frightened by Calder
And maybe by Henri Matisse.

One person only
Could quiet his crying,
Restore him, and render him happy,
And that was his granny
Whose neck and whose jowls
Had latterly grown rather crepey.

She'd lean down to coo
And the same baby who
Was possessed by the Goblin Depravity
Would gurgle and giggle
To see her flesh jiggle
When subject to forces of gravity.

She'd lift him to hold
And he'd grab at the folds
She had marked for cosmetic improvement;
But now she was stuck,
She was fresh out of luck:
Her grandson was calmed by their movement.

She can't understand
Why it's part of God's plan
That the back of one's hands should grow mottled,
But she's grasped and construed
Why, refreshed and renewed,
On Day Eight, He invented the wattle.

* "Frühlingsrauschen" is the original title of this parlour
piano classic by the Norwegian composer Christian
Sinding (1856–1941). Typically, it is translated as "Rustle
of Spring." I've taken liberties because this is one of those
occasions when accuracy must cede ground to scansion.

COME SEE!

Come see us off on the cruise ship,
Come see us off on the plane,
Come see us off in the German-built camper that
    occupies fully two lanes.
Come see our marvellous penthouse,
Come see the glorious view,
Come see the ways that we're spending the money
    you thought we were leaving to you.

Come see Par-ee in the springtime,
Come see the chestnut blooms swell,
Come see the way we've adapted to doormen and
    life in a five-star hotel.
Come see Palm Springs in December,
Come see the sparkling Azores,
Come see us winnow the pile of the savings you
    probably thought would be yours.

Come see us gathering rosebuds,
Come see us seizing the day,
Come see us living Mehitabel's motto, to wit:
    "Toujours gai, toujours gai."
Come see us drain your inheritance,
Come see the wages of sin,
Come see us laid in our custom-built caskets.
    We'll be the ones with the grins.

THE LATE ADAPTER

It was more than a little ironic
That his ma and pa named him Edison,
Since, from the draw of his very first breath,
He'd been disinclined to jettison
The things he knew,
The tried and true:
He showed no inclination
To warm to change,
Embrace the strange
Or welcome innovation.

He was firmly affixed to the analog.
He would never be caught extolling
The joys, for example, of power windows:
What was so hard about rolling?
Nor would he cave
To a micro-wave,
No, not if he won the lottery.
He'd never own
A Touch Tone phone:
He was fine, just fine, with rotary.

When hymns to computers were widely sung,
He wouldn't take part in the chorus,
Preferring, instead, his Remington Standard,
His Webster's, and Roget's Thesaurus.
Imagine, then,
Our great shock when,
Bereft of all breath and vigour,
We found him there,
In his favourite chair,
In the fulsome grip of rigor.

The iPhone he clutched in his stiffening paw
Was his granddaughter's, as it transpired.
Who knows what moved him to take his first selfie?
We just know he did, then expired.
We broke his grasp,
We looked, we gasped:
Oh jeepers, oh creepers, those peepers!
Those vacant eyes,
That hood, that scythe:
That photobomb prankster, Grim Reaper.

THE OLD MAN GIVES IN TO CHURLISHNESS

Look up!
Look up
From your life-and-death texting,
Look up!
Look up and you'll know
An angel rode by on a six-legged horse
Past the tropical birds in the snow.

WHO CAN'T GO ON, WHO MUST GO ON
(for Bill Pechet)

You're wide awake at 5 a.m.,
Or some ungodly hour.
The cactus you've had thirty years
Has just burst into flower.
You didn't know this kind of thing
Was even in its line;
Its repertoire, you always thought,
Was prickle, spike, and spine.

"Just look at what I made," it begs.
Your bleary-eyed inspection
Reveals a pink extrusion
Like a St. Bernard's erection.
The odour is astonishing:
It hauled you from your dreams,
This strange mélange of mango,
Sweaty jockstrap, curdled cream.

Were you inclined to keep a list
Called "Things I Can't Believe,"
You'd likely think to itemize
That this was up its sleeve.
It's rather like discovering
The child you thought was mute
Can sight-sing Dowland madrigals
And, what's more, play the lute.

Concerning cacti husbandry
Devoutly, you're a layman.
But nonetheless, you're fairly sure
The petals, stem, and stamen
That took the overnight express
And got off at this station
Would, rather than a long life,
Opt for one that's brief and fragrant.

You've got just one appointment,
Which is easily postponed;
Though no one ever thinks to call,
You disengage the phone.
And then you simply sit there.
You sit, that's all, that's it.
You sit there, sit there, sit there,
You just sit there, sit there. Sit.

You've got this decorative gong —
A gift — you sometimes ring,
But otherwise you just take in
The succulent's new bling.
Your Zen career is not long-lived:
The unexpected bloom
Is wilting fast by 10 a.m.
And black by half past noon.

Over and out. Signed off. Washed up.
All done. A wrap. No more.
Exotic wafts cede precedence
To cabbage rolls next door.
Now cactus is as cactus was:
Stolid, and squat, and plain.
You can't go on, you must go on:
It could always happen again.

ENVOI: TO THE YOUNG

No reason to worry,
No cause for alarm,
No need to be fretful or frightened;
It's pleasant enough
Sitting back on your duff
Counting pills
While your cataracts ripen.

BILL RICHARDSON is a writer and broadcaster. His books include *Bachelor Brothers' Bed & Breakfast*, which won the Stephen Leacock Award for Humour, and *After Hamelin*, a novel for children, which won the Silver Birch Award. For CBC Radio, he hosted "Richardson's Roundup" and "Bunny Watson." He lives in Vancouver, B.C. and Holmfield, Manitoba.

ARS LONGA VITA BREVIS

ROXANNA BIKADOROFF is an award-winning Canadian artist whose illustrations have been published internationally for more than twenty-five years. Her illustrations have appeared in hundreds of magazines and newspapers, including *The New Yorker* and *The Walrus* magazine and on numerous book covers. She was born in Montreal and currently lives in Vancouver.